Andrew Tate Unshackled

Andrew Tate's Lessons from Jail

Dominic Steele

The Real World

Copyright © 2023 by The Real World

All rights reserved.

No portion of this book may be reproduced in any form without written permission from the publisher or author, except as permitted by U.S. copyright law.

Contents

Introduction	V
1. Lesson #1	1
2. Lesson #2	4
3. Disconnected from Power	7
4. Lessons from Scarcity	10
5. Lesson #5	12
6. Lesson #6	14
7. Lesson #7	17
8. Question from Jail #8	20
9. Lesson #9	22
10. Story from Jail #10	25
11. Lesson #11	29
12. Realities of Jail #12	31
13. Lesson #13	33
14. Lesson #14	36
15. Lesson #15	38
16. Lesson #16	40

17.	Lesson #17	42
18.	Lesson #18	44
19.	Lesson #19	47
20.	Lesson #20	50
21.	The Brutal Truth #21	53
22.	Newton's Third Law #22	58
23.	Blueprints, Plans and God #23	60
24.	What would your ancestors say? #24	63
25.	Release #25	65
26.	Conclusion	72

Introduction

In a world filled with limitations and invisible shackles, there exist remarkable individuals who defy expectations, break barriers, and transcend the ordinary. Andrew Tate is one such extraordinary soul. His life has been a relentless pursuit of freedom, power, and the unapologetic assertion of self.

"Lessons from Jail" is not just a book; it's a chronicle of an epic journey that took place within the confinements of a 3-meter cell. It's an unfiltered revelation of what transpires when a powerful mind clashes with an insurmountable obstacle.

This gripping narrative unveils the harsh reality of incarceration and the unparalleled insight Andrew gained during 96 days of seclusion. It's a raw, unfiltered account of a man who refused to be broken and emerged from the crucible stronger, wiser, and more determined than ever.

As you flip through these pages, you'll be transported into the heart of that dimly lit cell. You'll feel the emotions, the doubts, and the determination that swirled within. You'll be exposed to the harsh truths about life and the ruthless grip that society maintains over our destinies.

"Lessons from Jail" delves into the paradox of hope and its power to either liberate or trap us. It's an exploration of how strategic planning, unwavering diligence, inexhaustible patience, and unwavering spirit can propel us from the depths of despair to the peaks of redemption.

For those who dare to dream beyond the boundaries, who yearn for a life of true power, and who refuse to be prisoners of circumstance, this book is your compass.

Chapter One

Lesson #1

The human mind is not well adapted to absolute boredom.

This makes jail the ultimate training ground for emotional control.

I've seen men cry happiness over a coca-cola.

I've seen people get angrily attacked over a cigarette.

Emotions are the original entertainment.

In the outside world, you do not realize how entertaining emotions are.

How addicting the feeling is

Being happy,

Sad,

Angry,

You feel them, but your constant external distraction of work, your phone and other stimulus diminishes the extent.

It is very easy to be stoic when you are entertained by something else.

In jail,

Where distractions are so limited.

Emotions become the entertainment of choice for most.

Inmates ENJOY feeling anger,

They entertain themselves with pure feelings of happiness or sadness.

I've seen men fight the guards for pure fun.

Men argue in blistering anger over the pronunciation of a name.

Men crying for hours then laughing in hysteria.

It is an animal house.

I am grateful

It is the perfect testing ground for my zen.

Day 53.

My Iron Mind remains unphased.

- Tate

Chapter Two

Lesson #2

How many of you have genuinely tried to fly?

GENUINELY.

How many of you have researched, trained, and truly TRIED to fly?

NONE OF YOU.

Why?

Because you think it's impossible.

You've never pushed yourself because you believe the goal can never be achieved.

You've never even TRIED,

Imagine how much harder some men would work if it was possible.

The amount of work ethic inspired by witnessing a man train his arms to move so hard and fast that he could fly.

There is power in knowing something is possible.

I was put on this earth by God himself to show you what is possible.

You are not meant to be a slave.

I was poorer than you,

I was raised in a council estate by a single mother.

I made it out.

I conquered the internet.

I became The Top G.

They cannot keep me in this cell forever.

My enemies' lies are crumbling.

This is your time to play catch up.

Whatever situation you are in, I want to let you know one thing is certain.

It is possible.

Get to work.

- Tate

Chapter Three

Disconnected from Power

Your electronic devices are a fundamental part of you.

It's been nearly 30 days since I've interacted with an electronic device

and my thoughts are louder than ever before.

Like a newly blind man who develops an acute sense of smell, touch, and hearing.

I had unlimited information and communicative powers which I could conjure into my hands at will.

I've been cut off, but you haven't.

You reading this possess UNLIMITED power at your disposal.

If you're broke you can learn what to do to become rich.

If you're weak you can learn what to do to become strong.

You have instant and continuous access to every good and bad idea thought up.

You do not have the same problem as your ancestors.

When your grandparents were broke, they couldn't just listen to a rich person on how to make money.

When they wanted to become better fighters, they couldn't just google their nearest fight gym.

You have UNLIMITED POWER.

You are only weak, poor, or alone because you do not use the power at your fingertips.

If you can read this email, you can find any tool you need with a few clicks.

You stand on the shoulders of giants.

Get to work.

- **Tate**

Chapter Four

Lessons from Scarcity

Caffeine is a miracle.

Nearly 30 days stuck inside this dungeon and I've learned some truths about life.

Nearly 30 days without a single drop of caffeine and I can tell you that a caffeinated life is a better life.

Nothing GOOD has come from my lack of caffeine.

My days are slightly less alert but it's no easier for me to fall asleep every night.

Coffee powered the entire industrial age.

The coffee break became a staple in business because a caffeinated business outcompetes a non-caffeinated business.

Remember this whenever you see some nerd order decaf coffee.

I'm perspicacious enough to monitor the results a lack of caffeine has brought to my life.

There is no advantage.

Start your morning with TWO plain black coffees and conquer your day.

Don't listen to the psy-op saying two coffees in the morning is bad for you.

The Matrix wants you weak, poor, and alone.

I communicate my lessons to you so that you may become strong, rich, and surrounded by brothers.

Empowerment of the average man is my only crime.

Start your mornings caffeinated.

Such is the Way of Wudan.

- Tate

Chapter Five

Lesson #5

I can feel your energy.

They have extended my imprisonment another 30 days in an attempt to break me.

But they misunderstand,

I cannot be broken because they need to break all of us first.

Top G is an idea.

You cannot lock it up.

It's the idea that men should strive to be their best selves.

That they should be strong, honorable, and diligent.

All of my content,

All of my messages,

Are designed to light the suppressed fire in every man.

A fire society often tries to extinguish.

You shouldn't be content being average.

You should strive to be the best version of yourself possible,

To take care of your loved ones,

Innovate and spark your genius,

And become great.

The idea of Top G cannot be broken,

The Truth will win.

When I am released, I will see who truly was on my team.

Who truly supports the idea of Top G.

- Tate

Chapter Six

Lesson #6

If I asked you who you would like to be in your ideal life.

Would the answer be who you are now?

YES OR NO

"I wanted to be a fighter, an astronaut, a firefighter, a billionaire, but instead I'm an accountant."

THEN YOU ARE A COWARD.

You KNEW what you wanted to be.

But you didn't even TRY to become it.

Maybe you'll have never succeeded in being a fighter pilot, professional fighter, or billionaire.

But if you TRIED as hard as you could.

You'd likely have been in more planes, more fights, and run more businesses than you have now.

You'd be CLOSER to your goal.

Failure is fine.

The CLOSER you are. The better.

You don't NEED the end goal to feel happiness.

To feel accomplishment and purpose.

So the question is.

Why aren't you trying?

You will have a myriad of bullshit answers.

There's this really stupid answer which people think sounds good...

"I'm scared of failure"

Shut up.

You're an idiot.

I just explained how even if you fail, you're closer to what you want to be.

The pure momentum and effort attributed to the direction of your dreams can ONLY be a net positive.

You're SCARED of what?? A net positive?

STOP BEING A COWARD.

Wanna be a UFC champion? GOOD.

Go to a fight gym. TODAY.

Will you ever make it? Don't know.

But you'll be able to fight better a year from now than if you didn't go.

You have no more excuses.

- Tate

Chapter Seven

Lesson #7

My cell is spotless.

Absolutely organized and optimized.

It's out of principle.

Out of habit.

Professionalism is a life choice.

Sloppiness in one area of life results in sloppiness in all areas of your life.

Sloppiness is a mindset.

When you live your life in constant mess and disorganization.

How can you expect to be a professional at anything else?

You can't even get your life in order.

How are you going to conquer earth?

You don't even walk professionally.

Genuinely.

When you walk anywhere, are you moving as smoothly as possible to get from point A to point B?

Are you walking **WITH PURPOSE?**

Whenever I meet a man, I look at how smoothly he moves through life.

If I tell him to add me to his contacts, does he know EXACTLY where the app is?

Does he blunder typing in his passcode?

Flip through his phone, searching back and forth for the app?

Is he sloppy?

Sloppy in one aspect, is sloppiness in all aspects of life.

I won't work with him.

He'll fuck up, he's a liability.

True Professionals understand that EVERYTHING can be done at a professional standard.

There's a right and a wrong way to breathe.

And you think it doesn't matter that your closet is a disorganized mess.

Sloppy in one aspect, is sloppiness in all aspects.

You now get to decide, if you'll keep living the life of an amateur just like everyone else.

- Tate

Chapter Eight

Question from Jail #8

Here are some uncomfortable truths about yourself.

You are only so comfortable living without an edge because you've never exploited one in the first place.

Complacent and happily "progressing" through life at a snail's pace.

You've never ONCE pushed yourself to the true physical or mental limit.

Never once truly displayed absolute brilliance.

You've been coasting through life and semi-failing forever.

A dim lightbulb, forever on.

Not entirely off, but never truly on.

Losing while watching me and those around me ENDLESSLY WIN for years.

Every day you wake up and lie to yourself that you're actually TRYING to become something of value in life.

And you know it's a lie.

That's the difference between me and you,

I'm brutally honest with myself.

Look yourself in the mirror again and ask,

Are you even TRYING?

- Tate

Chapter Nine

Lesson #9

The secret to money-making is time.

Jail is weaponized to try and rob you of it,

If you're reading this and you want to become wealthy,

You need to understand this principle.

Time must be spent on one of two outcomes.
1) Money saved.
2) Money made.

A company hires an accountant because the amount of money spent is less than the amount of money saved.

A company hires a worker because the amount of money spent is less than the amount of money made.

The company is buying their employees time.

It then sells its employees' time for a profit.

When you are purchasing a product, you are buying TIME.

A good purchase saves or makes you more time than it costs.

If you make $100 per hour, why would you not spend $10 to save an hour?

These opportunities pass you by every day,

TIME is everything.

When you understand this,

You will spend your time wisely.

Every second you waste.

Every moment you let go by,

Every missed opportunity,

You are spending the only resource you have.

The only thing that matters.

TIME.

- Tate

Chapter Ten

Story from Jail #10

There is one story that visits me very often in this cell.

Atop Wudan in the year 109, Master Po took me to the cliff's edge.

"The first lesson in Zen is about mortality," he said.

"When you reach my level of power, you know exactly when you will die."

He produced a handful of pink apple blossoms from his robe and threw them into the wind - they floated upon the breeze, scattering into the valley two miles below.

"Retrieve every last blossom.

And when you have picked up the very last one, you will know that I have passed to the next life."

I bowed and shed a tear.

Then began my walk down the mountain.

I found the first blossom two weeks later.

Laying in a rock pool, bright pink contrasting violet blue.

I lived in the wilderness, hunting wolves with handmade weapons, and spent every waking hour searching for the blossoms.

I had no desire to hasten his passing, yet I understood to always obey.

After 21 years, I had found 99 of the 100 blossoms.

I had walked over 3000 miles through wilderness.

The mountain winds had blown them far and wide.

I spent another 60 years, looking for the final piece.

I would meditate at night to keep frustration at bay and spend my days sifting through dirt, climbing trees and swimming lakes - knowing the blossom could be anywhere.

The final blossom eluded me.

I dreamt of it. I hallucinated. I saw it permanently in my mind, but could never find it.

And then... 81 years after first descending from the mountain, I came across a large flat rock.

Upon it was the perfect imprint of an apple blossom.

The piece must have landed here many years ago, and the blistering sun had all but obliterated it - leaving nothing but the perfect print on hard stone.

I was furious.
So many years wasted. Elements endured.

And it's now clear, I could never complete the task.
I returned to Wudan with 99 blossoms to find Po meditating.

I knelt before him and began to cry through frustration.

"I have failed. I did not move quickly enough for the sun. I will never have all of the blossoms."

He smiled and replied. "Then I will never die."

Such is The Way Of Wudan

Chapter Eleven

Lesson #11

Jail is a fantastic way to see who is actually on your team.

Most men in here have phone calls but no one to call.

No letters to read.

All of them have a family.

Every inmate had some friends.

But Jail is a strong test.

And most men chose their team poorly. They failed.

Every one of you reading this, Ask yourself.

How would your team perform if you were imprisoned? If they would perform poorly.

Work to change that.

You cannot be rolling with cowards.

Everyone has friends when the sun shines.

But you will need your friends most when it rains. You cannot conquer the world alone.

I will emerge from jail as a better person.

But a better person needs better people.

My team may be enjoying freedom,

But the burden to increase in diligence, competence and professionalism is shared by us all.

Such is The Way of Wudan

Chapter Twelve

Realities of Jail #12

Locked in a box.

Blistering cold.

Three cement walls and a steel door.

You hear how your family misses you.

You do not know what tricks your enemies will pull.

Completely innocent.

But no freedom.

Yells and screams are the only music in here.

You're given a pencil, paper and a single book.

24 hours a day.

Everyday.

You wake up in the same familiar place.

But it could always be worse. Depression isn't real.

- Tate

Chapter Thirteen

Lesson #13

Jail brings clarity.

All there is to do is think about how reality works.

No man became a World Level Opponent on "accident" Excellence doesn't just magically happen.

It's not smooth, It's not easy.

It doesn't just fall into place.

It is **INTENTIONAL.**

You will not meet who you **NEED** to meet by accident.

You will not have everything you want in life naturally.

You must **WILL** it into existence through sheer grit.

You don't just magically make it to the winner's table.

You pave your way in.

The idea that passivity works is cope.

Cope for the men who do not want to **TRY**.

Cope for COWARDS afraid of risk.

Do not believe the lies losers spread.

They do not know the amount of intention, action, AND RISK it takes to do anything remarkable.

It will never fall into place.

You need to WORK to PUT IT into place.

You need to pave your way to the winners' table.

And then you need to prove you deserve to stay there.

My father used to play chess over the phone.

No board,

He used the board in his mind and recited the moves he wanted to make over the telephone to his opponent.

I am on day 25 of my daily mental chess game.

I lost the board position on move 16 today.

It is not smooth. It is not easy.

But when I exit this cell.

I will be able to play like my father did.

I will surpass the need for a chessboard.

What will you have accomplished by the time I leave this cell?

I will be out soon.

Tick Tock.

- Tate

Chapter Fourteen

Lesson #14

God puts hardship in your path to give you an opportunity to show him just how strong you can be.

Martin Luther King Jr.

Malcolm X.

Nelson Mandela.

Serving Jail time with full innocence is a badge of honor.

I serve my time understanding this,

It's a test.

It's an opportunity.

It has been over 5,000 years since I last spent 96 hours straight practicing the Ki-zami-zuki technique.

Many of you reading this right now may be suffering hardship. Life as a man will always be full of it.

I send you these letters to remind you,

Enjoy the rain while it lasts,

Enjoy the storms,

The chaotic seas.

It is temporary.

It is an opportunity

Calm seas never made a skillful sailor.

Smile through the struggle.

Use it to become great.

- Tate

Chapter Fifteen

Lesson #15

Don't take mindset tips from the happy man.

Take them from the depressed miserable man who performs exceptionally.

Everybody can preach positivity in the sunshine.

A **CHILD** can be happy when things are going well.

I learned mindset from my kickboxing coach as he cried telling me stories of the genocide in Bosnia.

As my father held his fractured face together.

I paid attention to his words.

These are LESSONS.

THIS IS MINDSET.

Everyone can smile in the club.

Smile when your nose is broken.

THAT'S A MAN.

Most men are living life on easy mode.

Talking about being a lifeguard in 6 inches of water.

It's the men in the stormy seas who have lessons to teach.

Not the forever-smiling dork.

- Tate

Chapter Sixteen

Lesson #16

It is extremely important as a man that you become rich.

Because money is power.

And power is required in the never-ending battle against evil.

Dedicate yourself to God and become as rich as possible.

Every day in this cell, I train.

I work. I write.

I prepare for my release.

Every one of you must be doing the same.

Train hard. Work hard.

Become as powerful as possible.

Do not get outperformed by me in a cell.

This is your golden opportunity to catch up.

The battle against evil is never-ending.

If you are on the forces of good.

It is your duty to become as powerful as possible.

- Tate

Chapter Seventeen

Lesson #17

Much like life, prison is a battle against doubt.

Every one of you is fighting the same fight.

It's a battle that must be fought and won in order to reach the peaks of greatness.

Doubt is insidious and creeping.

Thick and poisonous.

It aims to engulf and constrict your mind cutting off your ability to perceive the light.

Many of you reading this, have doubts.

Doubt you can become great.

Doubt of what is actually possible for you to achieve.

But you need to destroy it.

Doubt is not your ally.

It is a poison that spreads, You must get rid of it absolutely.

I am from government housing, I'm from the bottom of the socio-economic ladder.

I achieved all my successes despite every statistic saying I would fail.

Doubt was all around me.

But I never once adopted it.

The destruction of doubt is one of the many secrets of Wudan.

I became a master 2,973 years ago. You must train and become the same.

- Tate

Chapter Eighteen

Lesson #18

The entire world is a game.

A battle of ideas.

Jail is what can happen to people who try to change the world.

An unfortunate possible outcome of playing the game.

When you make a roll of the dice Sometimes it will go well Sometimes it will not, It's Monopoly.

You put it on the dice, Sometimes the dice roll good, Sometimes they roll bad, Go directly to jail, do not pass Go, do not collect $200.

The spectator may laugh.

But the player has another chance, It's part of the game, An unfortunate possibility of being a player in the Arena.

Spectators never need to worry.

Jail won't happen to the man stacking grocery shelves, Jail won't happen to the man cleaning cars.

Jail won't happen to the men who don't play the game.

Jail is an unfortunate possible outcome for men trying to make a change.

Martin Luther King Jr. Malcolm X Nelson Mandela, And more.

They were given some bad rolls, But you still remember their name.

Great players of the game.

The spectator will cheer and boo, watch the entire show.

But no one will remember him, He's not playing the game, he's only watching it.

One day I will be released because I've done nothing wrong.

I'm not a criminal, I have not broken the law.

I'm a player of the game trying to change the world for the better.

The Truth will win.

And I will continue to positively influence the world.

Remember the name, **TATE.**

Chapter Nineteen

Lesson #19

We all have our favorite emotions.

The ones we default to and seek.

This is why junkies are junkies.

Why athletes are athletes.

Why winners win and losers lose.

Everybody wants that familiar feeling.

Whether it's a good feeling.

Or a bad one.

My default feeling is proud.

I enjoy feeling better than everyone around me with undeniable empirical evidence.

Hottest girl, strongest team, iron minded, whatever.

I love to FLEX.

Searching for my favorite feeling has built me an EXCEPTIONAL life.

It's FORCED me to make something I can be proud of.

What's your feeling? If it's "happy" that's just as destructive as "sad" And trust me.

Some people WANT to feel sad.

Perpetual victims.

But happiness is the hedonistic highway to addictions.

Short-sighted.

Drink this vodka, take this pill, eat that cake, I want to feel HAPPY YAY.

Society has conditioned men to believe we should be happy.

We are not children.

Life is not a playground.

"There's something wrong with you if you're not happy"

WRONG.

I know successful dedicated brilliant men who are not giggling like little girls.

Fuck happy.

Chase more.

Be more.

Be great.

- Tate

Chapter Twenty

Lesson #20

In chess, the Check forces you to move.

If you didn't - you'd be dead the next turn.

So you waste a move, waste a precious moment in time.

You lose tempo.

You fall behind.

Your opponent seizes the momentum.

Then you die.

Life has been checking you your entire life, you haven't protected yourself.

A Check is a consequence of failing to preempt attacks.

CHECK.

Now you can't travel.

CHECK.

Now you can't use your bank account.

CHECK.

Your girl leaves you.

CHECK.

Your employer fires you.

CHECK.

You could've stopped all of these if you protected yourself.

In chess, the King protects himself with Knights, Rooks, Bishops, Pawns, and the Queen.

He would die if he played the game alone.

Do you understand?

- Tate

Chapter Twenty-One

The Brutal Truth #21

When I was 8, I lost a winning game at a chess tournament.

It was an 11 hours drive to get there, and I blundered and lost a winning position.

I told my father it was because I was tired and couldn't sleep in the car.

I came third in the tournament but should have come first.

Dad was furious.

I remember feeling like crying as he lectured me.

"Who taught you to make excuses boy? It wasn't me. Isn't your last name Tate?

What does the paper say?

Lost cause he was tired? Or LOST?"

I didn't reply.

"Answer me, son!"

It says I lost dad.

"Excuses don't affect the outcome.

So excuses can't affect your performance."

I was too young to understand and upset.

When we got home, I complained to mom that dad was yelling at me for losing.

She said he was too hard on me.

They had a heated argument as he explained she's a female and doesn't understand the burden of performance.

"IF I WAS TOO TIRED TO PERFORM, THEY WOULD HAVE KILLED ME"

He was referencing a few months before where I watched him be attacked.

My mother told me I didn't have to play chess anymore if dad was going to upset me.

Dad took me out of the house for a week.

We stayed in a hotel away from my mother's influence.

He kept me up playing chess till the early hours. 2/3 am.

6 am school. Every night of the week.

"Your dad's crazy" mother would say.

In fact, everyone said that.

At the time I didn't know who to believe.

But I was exhausted. I cried a few times.

He made me play anyway.

And made me sleep very little before school.

I remember on day 5 or 6 of this sitting across the board.

He had set up a position, white to win in 7 moves.

After a few minutes, I found the winning combination. A knight sacrifice.

Dad cheered.

"DAMN SON! That's a master puzzle!"

I was excited and happy.

"You're more tired now than you were in that tournament, ain'tcha?"

"Tired isn't an excuse son. What's your last name?"

Tate I replied.

"Tired or not, you know how to win"

My dad sacrificed his marriage to raise me exceptionally. My mother simply didn't get it.

Men raise pussy sons because they cuck to wives.

My father lost his wife for **ME.**

I always used to remember this story when deep in the rounds of championship fights.

Am I gonna lose because I'm tired? Or just lose.

Tates know how to win.

- Tate

Chapter Twenty-Two

Newton's Third Law #22

Everybody wishes they were me when I'm in my Bugatti.

But no one wishes they were me when I'm incarcerated.

Newton's Third Law.

For every action, there is an equal and opposite reaction.

Exceptional doesn't always mean good, it means far from average.

Everyone is too afraid to lose,

To ever win.

You cannot just become a billionaire from government housing,

You cannot just become the most googled man on the planet,

Without a reaction.

There was no way to avoid what has happened to me.

You cannot just become it without attracting the haters,

The attacks.

You cannot become a world influence without creating very powerful enemies.

I will be freed when the truth comes to light.

- Tate

Chapter Twenty-Three

Blueprints, Plans and God #23

Skyscrapers are never built by accident.

Amazing things are not luck.

You're a feather in the wind - direction decided by outside forces.

Your emotions. Your boss.

You have zero engines to **POWER** yourself.

Here's how you fix it:

First, you need to identify your current position.

Most of you have NO idea what your current position is. You're blind.

Ok. You know your job and car.

You don't know how much your car is worth, or what other people with the same job are getting paid at the neighboring company.

Before you make a move you need to know - **WHERE AM I?**

Look at the chessboard and SEE your strengths and weaknesses before you decide which move to make.

Strengths. Weaknesses. Commitments. Liabilities. Assets.

Then you need to make a plan to minimize the negatives and promote the positives.

Take a personal strength you have and ask yourself.

Is there ANY other way I can use said strength besides how it's already being used?

Writing goals are easy.

Writing steps on how you achieve each goal using the strengths you've identified is realistic.

Realistic and easy rarely go hand in hand.

Goals mean nothing without a plan.

A destination without a map is wish wash BULLSHIT.

Stop BULLSHITTING yourself.

You bullshitted yourself your entire life and it got you NOWHERE.

Strengths.

Weaknesses.

Previous successes/failures.

Goals and ways to achieve utilizing strengths.

This is the BASIC outline.

You need to follow it rigorously.

- Tate

Chapter Twenty-Four

What would your ancestors say? #24

God tests his favorite creations with the hardest battles.

It is an opportunity to show God how strong you are.

It's an audition to showcase your brilliance.

I am human,

I miss my family,

I miss my freedom.

But I also understand.

Life as a man is struggle and pain.

I will continue to write and work in this cell.

I will continue to prepare for my eventual release.

My ancestors are watching me.

I will show them.

I am outstanding even in the rain.

To all of you with your own trials and struggles.

I recommend you do the same.

Perform exceptionally despite the rain.

- Tate

Chapter Twenty-Five

Release #25

While sitting in jail... there were many thoughts that permeated my mind.

Incessant and persistent, some more enjoyable than others.

I could use my Iron Mind to destroy them absolutely and force more manageable contemplation.

But...

Sometimes, in places of absolute difficulty, you should allow the thoughts and feelings that come.

They are messages from the universe.

So I opened the iron door, and allowed myself to think what I thought.

Some days I would be hopeful, others pessimistic.

Both had advantages and disadvantages,

it was difficult to decide which mindset I truly preferred.

So, the universe decided to tell me.

I was stuck inside of a 3-meter cell, 24-hour a day lockdown, zero yard time...

Lock yourself in your bathroom without your phone or laptop and try to sit for an hour.

Then try 96 days.

After about 5 weeks I had the ability to finally choose a movie to watch.

I picked The Shawshank Redemption.

That movie hits differently from inside a jail cell.

Red said something while discussing the suicide of Brooks.

"These walls are funny. First you hate 'em, then you get used to 'em.

Enough time passes, you get so you depend on them. That's institutionalized."

That is the Matrix.

On a long enough time frame... many grow to love it.

In the movie, they talk about how institutionalized men are the ones who have given up all hope.

Red says "Hope is a dangerous thing. Hope can drive a man insane"

He's explaining how Jail (The Matrix) is easier to accept if you understand that you will never escape.

As soon as you believe there is another way, you feel pain. You feel frustration.

And this is the difference between pessimism and optimism.

If you truly believe you are screwed, the system is against you and you'll never get out,

A strange sense of calm comes over you.

You feel comfortable with inaction because it doesn't matter anyway, does it?

When I accepted I may never get out of prison, I felt BETTER.

Isn't that insane?

When I was optimistic and hopeful that I was innocent I would look at the walls around me and feel terrible.

The hope made me feel worse.

I would make frustrated phone calls and read legal books and think of the best possible way to defend myself.

But, now I am free.

Maybe if I didn't make those phone calls, I wouldn't be.

Sure, if I had stayed defeated I would have felt better inside the cell.

BUT I WOULD STILL BE INSIDE OF THE CELL.

I NEEDED the pain and NEEDED the frustration to escape.

If you truly want to achieve the impossible, you need to be hopeful that you can finally be free

and you need to feel angry that you are still inside your prison cell.

A lot of you may think you're not in a prison cell.

In jail, they decided when I woke up, when I slept, when I ate, and where I went.

In your life, your boss decides when you wake up and when you eat and your bank decides where you go.

You're in jail.

You are not free.

If you believe there is no way to escape you'll instantly feel better.

Like I did while I was pessimistic inside the jail cell.

If you believe you can escape you'll become temporarily enraged... but you WILL escape.

You need to feel the blood in your veins accelerate as you look at those who live outside of all conceivable parameters

while you are ABSOLUTELY AVERAGE.

The most beautiful women on the planet and the most important men on the planet have precisely zero desire to speak to you.

You couldn't pay them to waste their time because you are INSIDE of a jail cell.

You've never been free.

What could you possibly know? What stories could you possibly have?

You are INSIDE of the Matrix.

These people design the Matrix.

They build your life and they control your life.

They have zero desire to interact with you.

You do not matter.

And you will never matter unless you become free.

The true story of The Shawshank Redemption is one of optimism versus pessimism.

Red, who is negative, is shown by Andy, who is positive - that even impossible odds can be overcome with careful planning, diligence, patience and HOPE.

Andy struggled in jail.

But Andy escaped from jail.

Red was too much of a coward to feel the true pain of enslavement - and this is why, he remained enslaved for so long.

Do you understand what I am trying to say to you?

Careful planning. Diligence. Patience and Hope.

- **Tate**

Chapter Twenty-Six

Conclusion

Your Journey Begins Here:

As you turn the last page of "Unchained" a new chapter unfolds. This is not the end; it's just the beginning of your adventure. You've journeyed alongside a man who defies limits, and now it's time to carve your own path.

Your Path to Freedom:

With these lessons etched in your soul, you hold the keys to unlocking your potential. The walls that once hemmed you in will crumble, and the shackles that held you back will disintegrate. Your dreams and aspirations are within arm's reach, and your voyage to a life of fulfillment and prosperity has commenced.

Empower Others:

But why halt the transformation here? If the trials and triumphs of Andrew Tate have profoundly touched your life, they can do the same for others. Your review can be the guiding star for someone seeking a change. Share your experiences and ignite the spark in others to embark on their own transformative journey.

Leave a Review:

If "Unshackled" has inspired you, opened your eyes, or lit a fire within your soul, we humbly request a moment of your time to leave a review. Your words can be the catalyst for another person's breakthrough. By doing so, you become a beacon of inspiration for those on the cusp of their own transformation.

Thank You:

Thank you for choosing "Unchained" as your guide. We're eager to witness the heights you'll scale.

www.ingramcontent.com/pod-product-compliance
Lightning Source LLC
LaVergne TN
LVHW020911070425
807903LV00002B/287